I Walk a Frayed Tightrope Without a Safety Net

poems by

Carey Link

Finishing Line Press
Georgetown, Kentucky

I Walk a Frayed Tightrope Without a Safety Net

Copyright © 2021 by Carey Link
ISBN 978-1-64662-448-5 First Edition
All rights reserved under International and Pan-American Copyright Conventions.
No part of this book may be reproduced in any manner whatsoever without written permission from the publisher, except in the case of brief quotations embodied in critical articles and reviews.

ACKNOWLEDGMENTS

"I Walk a Frayed Tightrope Without a Safety Net"—*Awakening to Holes in the Arc of Sun* (Mule on a Ferris Wheel), *Poet's Choice*, Sundial Writers Corner on WLRH public radio, *The Birmingham Arts Journal*
"The Gift"—*Hospital Drive: The Literature and Humanities Journal of the UVA School of Medicine* at www.hospitaldrive.org
"Decoding the Colorless Puzzle"—*Birmingham Poetry Review, Poet's Choice*
"Illness"—*The Birmingham Arts Journal*
"The Last Stage"—This poem was written when I participated in the Writing The Journey writing workshop sponsored by the Living Beyond Breast Cancer Foundation in October of 2017. The poem was published at: http://www.lbbc.org/blog This piece has also appeared in *The Valley Weekly*.
"Benign or Malignant—This poem was published in the spring 2018 edition of *Months To Years* at http://www.monthstoyears.org, WLRH *Sundial Writers Corner, The Valley Weekly*, and Survivor's Review at www.survivorsreview.org
"My Time"—*Awakening to Holes in the Arc of Sun* (Mule on a Ferris Wheel)
"RX# 1140106"—*Quiet Storm Literary Magazine* at www.quietstormlitmag.com
"A Metaphor For Cancer"—*Through the Kaleidoscope* (Blue Light Press)
"To Walk a Frayed Tightrope"—*Through the Kaleidoscope* (Blue Light Press)

The poems "The Last Stage" and "My Time" are forthcoming in the anthology *Poets Speaking to Poets: Echoes and Tributes*

Publisher: Leah Huete de Maines
Editor: Christen Kincaid
Cover and Interior Art: Monica Yother, www.monicayother.com
Author Photo: Ashley Vaughn, www.whiterabbitstudios.com
Cover Design: Elizabeth Maines McCleavy

Printed in the USA on acid-free paper.
Order online: www.finishinglinepress.com
       also available on amazon.com

Author inquiries and mail orders:
Finishing Line Press
P. O. Box 1626
Georgetown, Kentucky 40324
U. S. A.

Table of Contents

I Walk a Frayed Tightrope without a Safety Net 1

The Gift (visual art) 2

The Gift 3

Chronic Signs 4

RX 1140106 5

A Multicolored Head Scarf 6

During a Round of Chemotherapy 7

Decoding the Colorless Puzzle 8

Benign or Malignant? 9

To Walk A Frayed Tightrope 10

A Metaphor for Cancer 11

The Appointment 12

Relapse 13

Tattoo 14

The Last Stage 15

Illness 16

My Time 17

For Dr. Marshall Schreeder, my oncologist at Clearview Cancer Institute in Huntsville, Alabama. On the day I was diagnosed with breast cancer, I asked you if I was going to die. You simply told me to life my life and let you worry about the rest. Thank you!

In memory of my friend Barbara Mangini, who dealt with metastatic breast cancer for several years. She told me I have won through perseverance and strength, despite this disease. She was one of the people who gave me strength.

In memory of Eula Battle. We shared our journey with cancer. She was a teacher and mentor, who left an indelible impression on the Huntsville Community,

I Walk a Frayed Tightrope Without a Safety Net

1.

I find 5 centimeters after a shower.
It's wiry diffuse, bilateral, inoperable…
What did I miss?
What was I doing in the months it took to multiply?

2.

Who are the shadows I will meet?
What are the signs—
colors—languages—passages
customs—traditions—
How will they change in a breath?

A conversation with Hercules and Apollo—
A toss in the arid open.

The Gift

Time is measured in rounds—
as the river drips through a curved, twisted catheter—
into indigo—cool bitter.

Side effects, signs, lists, codes, colors, acronyms—
try to read the colorless puzzle.

Stories of where it has traveled…

Closed eyes toss and flutter,
a bowed head,
a hand held.

He serves me an "Appletini"—I laugh.

I pick out a hand-made
teal scarf and a sky blue hat with a butterfly.

Chronic Signs

A relentless nomad
leaves a code of colors
where he travels.

My battle rhythm is a collection of chemotherapy—
I remember by an IV drip,
size, shape, color—
and the number of months it worked.

RX # 1140106

Somewhere on a high wire
I slide with ambidextrous hands up, down, though, side-to-side
grasping for round edges of breath one second at a time
Poison is my shadow—
a hieroglyphic stranger—a 365 ritual of rounds for life—
a treasure hunt I want to hide and lose.

A Multicolored Head Scarf

My head is a Fortune Teller's map—
of intersected veins and bones.

Where a furrowed field waits to grow—

I have chosen to wear

azure, yellow rose,
orange sun,
and indigo sky

down my back.

During a Round of Chemotherapy

You sit across from me—
as an IV drip
spirals through my veins.

Our eyes close
at the same time.

Decoding the Colorless Puzzle

I can't hear—remember—feel—taste—smell—touch the systemic
    hieroglyphic
who hangs in my hourglass house.

I'm learning the languages of rounds sifted, tossed into days, weeks,
    hours—
milligrams, diameter, distribution, red, and the *o* of my held breath…

Where are the next smoke signals?

Benign or Malignant?

I've memorized protocol:

Name: Carey Link
Date of Birth: 2-12-75
Last 4 of social: XXXX

Pass.

Bitter-sour
of saline hangs—

I give three vials
of O-.

Pass.

Freeze.

A new typography on the right at 1:00.
What are the shapes of its curves—signs—symbols?

I hear a crooked, homeless puzzle of half-syllables without strings.
I play Hang Man with strangers.

To Walk a Frayed Tightrope

I swing over holes with my eyes closed—
to glide on the roundness of a breath,
and balance on the edges

of asymmetrical curves.

A Metaphor for Cancer

Cancer is a crooked road without signs.
Where the ground shifts without warning,
and I swing-swerve on the edges
of its asymmetrical curves—

into the arid open.
I feel betrayed by my body.
I'm not going to win.

The Appointment

The cane of a question mark
hangs in my hourglass house.
I feed, sift,
strain, fold
secrets that rise from beneath its floor—
concentric and evergreen.

How many turns are there
before mirage is a wasteland?

Relapse

My hourglass house sits in the corner,
moves side-to-side, up, down, around—
as I walk a frayed tightrope between seven suns
that swaddle clouds and bathe them red.

They find another piece of the breathing colorless puzzle.

The Tumor is ductal with lobular features.

I run an asymmetrical, crooked maze without signs, in search of green.

Tattoo

Covered by a transparent sheet
of faded, blue triangles—
my knotted limbs
are shifted onto the table.

I choose a concentric tattoo
instead of green crosses.

Pieces of me disappear—
into the revolutions of a beam—
to leave a raised, red valley of intersected veins
on the right side of my chest.

The Last Stage

I try to read the colorless, asymmetrical hieroglyphics
in malignant, bilateral, inoperable…

My systemic silhouette sifts the sand in my hourglass house
through cycles of daylight and darkness.

He leads as we dance on a frayed tightrope.
He dares me to learn the routine as I go—
and jump over its holes with my eyes closed.

While I learn to breathe again.

Illness

In my country of colorless labyrinths
there are no windows or doors.

The ground shifts without warning.

Language is a code of syllables without strings.

The promise of a moment is intertwined in poison.

My Time
> ...*if you want me again look for me under your boot soles*
> —*Walt Whitman*

My time is growing russet.

Dress me in every color.

Sing me a song
of four o' clock twilight
when sky melts
a tapestry
orange, rose indigo…
into a silver glitter—
I've met thousands of these.

Let me smell the hair
of a newborn baby.

Feel my tributaries
of blue—
each a beginning.

Warm me with the memories
you whisper.

Let me swaddle you in return.

Additional Acknowledgements

I would like to thank Leah Maines of Finishing Line Press for her faith in my work. I am grateful to Kathleen Thompson and the members of the Huntsville Literary Association poetry workshop for their feedback on this poetry sequence. I appreciate the great endorsements from Diane Frank, Dr. Monita Soni, and Debbie Dempsey West

Carey Link lives in Huntsville, Alabama. In 2008, she graduated with a B.A. in psychology from the University of Alabama, Huntsville. Carey is living with Cerebral Palsy. In 2017, two years after developing metastatic breast cancer she medically retired from sixteen years working in civilian personnel and Equal Employment Opportunity as a civil servant on Redstone Arsenal.

Coping with her disabilities has taught Carey patience and gratitude. *I Walk a Frayed Tightrope Without a Safety Net*, a finalist in the 2019 Blue Light Press chapbook contest, was inspired by her journey with cancer. She has never stopped moving forward, and is working toward a Masters in counseling at Faulkner University. After she completes her degree it is Carey's goal to work with clients living with life-altering illnesses or conditions.

In 2011, Carey's poetry sequence titled, *What it Means to Climb a Tree*, was released by Finishing Line Press and in 2017 her poetry collection Awakening to *Holes in the Arc of Sun* (Mule on a Ferris Wheel) was awarded second place in the Alabama State Poetry Society Book of the Year contest. In 2020, Carey's Poetry collection, *Through the Kaleidoscope* was published by Blue Light Press.

Carey enjoys mentoring emerging writers with disabilities through The Handy, Uncapped Pen online program.

www.ingramcontent.com/pod-product-compliance
Lightning Source LLC
Chambersburg PA
CBHW050822090426
42737CB00022B/3476